Emotional Freedom Technique (EFT) Through the Chakras

Michael Hetherington
(L. Ac, Yoga Teacher)

Disclaimer
All material in this book is provided for your information only and may not be construed as medical advice or instruction. No action or inaction should be taken based solely on the contents of this information. Instead, readers should consult the appropriate health professionals on any matter relating to their health and well-being. The information and opinions expressed here are believed to be accurate, based on the best judgment available to the author. Readers who fail to consult with the appropriate health authorities assume the risk of any injuries. The publisher is not responsible for errors or omissions.

About the Author

Michael Hetherington is a qualified acupuncturist, health practitioner and yoga teacher based in Brisbane, Australia. He has a keen interest in mind-body medicine, energetic anatomy, nutrition and herbs, lifestyle design, yoga nidra and Buddhist style meditation. Inspired by the teachings of many he has learned that a light-hearted, joyful approach to life serves best.

www.michaelhetherington.com.au

Other Titles by this Author:

The Complete Book of Oriental Yoga
A journey into the 5 elements and yoga for the seasons

How to Do Restorative Yoga
Learn the art of a gentle yoga practice for deep relaxation

Chakra Balancing Made Simple and Easy
How to work with the Chakras for enhanced living

Increasing Internal Energy
Building energy from within to enhance daily life and strengthen our yoga practice

The Yin and Yang Lifestyle Guide
Yin and yang theory applied to modern living

Table of Contents

Introduction

The Emotional Freedom Technique (EFT) is a powerful and simple method of energetic healing. What enables this simple technique to work, at a deep level, is the direct association with the meridian energetic system commonly used in traditional Chinese medicine. In Chinese medicine it has been thoroughly observed, documented and explored that these meridians directly influence our dense physical body, our psychology and potentially our spiritual body. It is because we are working directly with these energetic meridians that we can directly access and heal the many levels of our being.

There are three fundamental layers, levels or dimensions to the human being - the physical body, the mental/emotional body and the spiritual body. When we become ill or unbalanced in some way, it is usually because there is a dysfunction in at least one of these levels. It can be a dysfunction that exists on just one level or it could be a dysfunction that radiates onto a multitude of levels. Therefore, in the treatment process, it is important to work with methods or systems of healing that address as many of these levels or layers as possible. This gives us a much greater chance at healing and restoring balance to these three levels of our being. More often than not, we treat a disease or an imbalance just on one level, and it may not be the level at which the dysfunction is actually occurring. For instance, we may have a rash or some sort of skin disease. We go to a health practitioner and we get prescribed some kind of cream for the rash. This cream aims to treat the dense physical level of the body, and it may appear to work for a few days or a few weeks, but if the rash or skin disease is manifesting because of a dysfunction in the mental/emotional level, then the rash will return. With all diseases or feelings of unbalance, it is ideal to use methods or systems that address all three levels at the same time. If we do this, then the rapid healing of any illness is 99.999% likely.

It must be mentioned that some serious and chronic diseases are simply unable to be cured within this lifetime, for it may be due to a karmic reason or simply because the body is old and in the process of degeneration. Yet, this doesn't mean one cannot find happiness and peace when affected by such an illness. Sometimes, an illness provides an opportunity to take a deeper look at life, and with the right guidance and support, peace within the spiritual body and within the mind can be found even if the physical body has become weak or ill. Therefore, it can be said that the most potent and influential layer of the human being is the spiritual layer. Often a whole re-contextualization occurs for the body and mind if the spiritual body is awakened to a higher state of being. Therefore, if you have come across a sickness or imbalance and you have not been able to correct it or heal it on the physical or mental level, then the best approach is the spiritual domain. How do you do this? It's involves the process of ongoing self-enquiry, meditation, working with very subtle energy (chakras, meridians, the field of consciousness, etc.), letting go of old belief systems, delving deeper into the meaning of life and questioning your relationship with life that allows for the re-contextualization to occur.

EFT, through the Chakras, uses EFT in a new and dynamic way by addressing all three layers of the human being. The physical body (muscles), the mental/emotional body (emotions) and the spiritual body (chakras) are addressed with this method, and therefore, the potential for deep and sustainable healing is dramatically increased.

One of the best things about this style of treatment is that it is FREE to practice, you can do it pretty much anywhere, and it takes about 5-10 minutes to tap through one particular chakra.

The aftereffects can be different for different people. The most common response to tapping through one chakra is a sense of deep relaxation soon afterwards. If you feel sleepy after tapping through the chakras, I would advise you to honor it and simply lie down for a few minutes and close your eyes. You will awaken when your body is ready. Also, the mind tends to quiet on its own after a session of tapping. If it becomes quiet, let it be quiet. Try not to fill it up with thoughts again, and simply allow space to reside inside naturally. Do not force anything after a session; just let nature take care of it.

I have found great benefit with this method, and I sincerely hope that it provides you with a breakthrough in your healing journey.

May all beings be happy!

What is EFT?

EFT is a simple method that involves tapping and stimulating acupuncture points around the head and upper torso with your fingertips while bringing to mind and voice the issue or problem of concern.

Acupuncture points are little pools of accumulated energy that are located on the meridians that run throughout the body. The meridians are described like rivers that distribute energy and life force around the body. In Chinese medicine they are called meridians, while the yogas of India call them nadi's. In traditional Chinese medicine they have identified 14 main meridians that come to the surface of the body and therefore can be directly worked with by the healer or the physician. It's important to note that there are potentially hundreds and maybe even thousands of these meridians running throughout the body, and the same can be said regarding the acupuncture points. However, it is not necessary to study and understand all of these points and meridians because it has been found that working with the main ones has an overall effect on this extensive network.

Scientists have had trouble identifying the anatomical locations of these meridians and because of this, many scientists often come to the decision that any practices that utilize acupuncture points or meridians are inconclusive and likely to be false. However, there are a number of scientists that are continuing to investigate the existence of meridians and acupuncture points. A Japanese scientist known as Dr. Motoyama has come up with a new hypothesis to explain the existence of the meridians and acupuncture points. He has theorized that within the extensive network of connective tissue is a fluid that harbors an electrical charge and that this electrically charged fluid creates a pathway of electrical activity, which could explain the existence of the meridian pathways.

In many of the previous scientific explorations, scientists utilized and explored cadavers or dead bodies to search for the meridians. However, the first thing that happens to a dead body is that the fluids are drained. Therefore, any chance of finding an electrically charged fluid in the connective tissue of a cadaver becomes impossible and therefore no evidence to support the meridians exist. Dr. Motoyama's work is still underway and it looks promising that his theory may contribute greatly to the field of knowledge regarding meridian pathways and acupuncture points.

Regardless of what science has come to conclude, many healers and physicians continue to work with the meridians and acupuncture points, often with great results. What the healer or physician working with the meridians is attempting to do in a treatment is to stimulate and encourage the smooth flow of life force energy and blood throughout the body, which also triggers the body's own healing mechanism. When the life force energy and blood are flowing smoothly, all organs and bodily systems are nourished and are able to function at optimal levels. In Chinese medicine and the yoga's, it is understood and believed that when the organs and energy is flowing smoothly through the system it naturally calms and steadies the energies of the mind. When both mind and body are calm and steady, the spiritual body opens (also known as the shen or heart) and can work through us effortlessly, guiding us through the process of self-realization.

Therefore, the healer is not looking to heal the body; they are only initiating a change or a shift in the body's own life force and blood flow, triggering the patient's own healing mechanism. Therefore, the healer is but a catalyst in the healing process.

With EFT we can become our own healers by working directly with these meridians and acupuncture points. When we tap on the acupuncture points, it triggers a flush of energy and blood throughout the meridians. What makes EFT unique compared to acupuncture or other energy medicine techniques is that it has a conscious mental/emotional component added, making it potentially an effective intervention treatment in a more counseling and psychological context.

When we bring up a particular emotion, feeling or stressful thought, the energy running throughout our meridians shift to reflect that state. Often traumatic experiences cause our meridians to go into an unbalanced or stressed state and as a direct consequence we feel emotionally stressed. The energy in the meridians shifts into a balanced or stressed state and then that shift of energy gives rise to unpleasant emotions, stressful feelings and negative thinking.

Once the stressful state occurs in the meridians due to a traumatic event, the meridians can easily become programmed that way and so when the thought of the traumatic event is brought up, the meridians return to that programmed state. That's why when we think of a past trauma, we instantly re-live that same feeling. Talking about it without addressing the underlying energetic imbalance in the meridians is often unfruitful and very slow going. However, if we address the energetic imbalance in the meridians that is related to the traumatic event as soon as possible, the emotional intensity of that stressed state dissolves and all associated unpleasant feelings, emotions and negative thoughts tend to disappear.

How does this happen? Firstly, we bring to mind a past traumatic event and we will quickly feel the unpleased energetic state that follows. We then want to acknowledge the unpleasantness. We don't want to avoid or suppress it because this doesn't resolve the issue. Then, we use some focused words and sentences while we tap on the acupuncture points. What we find is that after following this procedure over a number of minutes, the intensity of stress around the thoughts of the past traumatic event dissipates dramatically. In some cases, all emotional intensity around the event dissolves completely, right then and there.

When we tap on the acupuncture points while holding the trauma in mind, we are stimulating and re-organizing the meridians system to restore energetic balance, therefore "snapping it out" of its unbalanced, stressful state whenever the trauma is brought to the surface of the mind. After a series of sessions working with the EFT technique, that same person brings to mind the previous traumatic event, and there remains little to no emotional intensity or stress around that event.

It may sound like a lot to take in if you are new to this idea or way of looking at the meridian energetic system. If it doesn't make a lot of sense to you now, do not worry about it. Instead, I encourage you to simply try the EFT technique out for yourself because at the end of the day we are more interested in the results. For some of you this explanation will make sense and I would encourage you to share these ideas and practices with others. The more people that become aware of the meridians and the power of techniques like EFT, the more awake and conscious we all become.

Gary Craig is credited as one of the original founders of the EFT technique, and I encourage you to read up and explore his work for yourself. He offers the information and explanations of EFT for free on his website. (www.garythink.com)

There are also hundreds of videos on YouTube of people exploring this technique, and I also encourage you to check them out to become more familiar with the potential of this modality.

One video I would recommend in particular is by "thetappingman." Please put this into your internet browser to see his video regarding the tapping sequence. www.youtube.com/thetappingman

If you have any trouble understanding the basic explanations of the technique in this book, then please check out the resources listed. When you feel confident using it, then come back and try out the chakra clearing methods explored in this book.

The Chakras

The chakras are an energetic system explored deeply by the yogis in India. These chakras are part of the energetic makeup of all humans, and the chakras are not linked to any particular religion or sect. They simply exist, whether you believe it or not, it doesn't really matter. The Chakras are the main energy centers, like electrical power stations, and the meridians or nadi channels provide the extensive network that helps to distribute this energy.

Those who are sensitive enough to feel and study them work with energetic techniques and yoga postures to balance these energetic centers out. When these chakras become dysfunctional or impaired and are left for a long time, disease or sickness on the dense physical body becomes manifested. If one continues to balance and support the imbalance of these chakras, it allows for a higher potential of being to emerge - one with a higher capacity for health, knowledge and great insight. There are literally hundreds and hundreds of books written about these chakras, so I will not attempt to explain them in great detail here, but rather, I will provide a summery of these chakras so you can become more familiar with them. Many people tend to get caught up on the elaborate descriptions of these chakras as explained in books and the like. I suggest avoiding too much intellectualization regarding these chakras and instead focus more on experiencing them on a practical and energetic level so that you can come to a greater understanding from your own personal experience.

On the following pages is a summery of each of the seven chakras. It describes their location and their function.

1st Base Chakra (Pubic Bone, Base of torso)

This is one of the major energy stations. The first and second chakras are the primary energy stations that feed the other chakras. Conditions like chronic fatigue and adrenal exhaustion are due to the 1 and/or 2nd chakras being deficient in energy, blocked or totally scrambled.

To be fully in the physical world and in our bodies, this chakra needs to be functioning and spinning properly. This chakra is the center of our most ancient and tribal rhythm. It is our deepest connection to Mother Earth. It is our earthing rod, essentially, that grounds out any excess electro activity that we may have picked up throughout the day. It helps us to ground, stabilize and unscramble. It calms the mind and provides us with a deep sense of inner strength and confidence.

This is the chakra of drumming, of music, of dance, and of primary urges to run, jump, dance, sing and mate.

Base Chakra Summery

In Balance, Signs & Symptoms	Out of Balance, Emotional Signs & Symptoms	Out of Balance, Physical Signs & Symptoms
Basic survival needs met, feels supported by life, money comes easily, strong & stable	Constant fear, easily startled, very anxious about future or direction in life, always in debt or struggling with money, ungrounded, deep guilt	Weak legs, addictive and obsessive behaviors, adrenaline junkie, depression, ongoing constipation or diarrhea, fatigue

2nd Sacral Chakra / Womb / Dan Tien
(About 1 inch below the belly button)

This is the chakra of our truest potential. A womb-like center that carries our gifts and our wisdom through various lifetimes. When we are walking our soul's true path, this Chakra is alive, strong and powerful. It feeds us with great confidence and courage. It is strongly connected to our primal fire. It is our fire for life, to experience life, to share life, to create life, and to support life; hence its connection to the mother/baby energy of nourishment and support. This chakra center is also our powerhouse. If this area is functioning well, our overall energy field, our state of mind and the health of our entire system will be strong and positively influential. It is also where our internal energies are stored for later in life.

Sacral Chakra Summery

In Balance, Signs & Symptoms	Out of Balance, Emotional Signs & Symptoms	Out of Balance, Physical Signs & Symptoms
Healthy sexuality, enjoyment of the physical, energetic & motivated	Guilt and shame around sexuality, perversion, obsessed with sex or lacks sex drive	Bladder & kidney problems, fertility issues, sexual organ problems, fatigue

3rd Solar Plexus Chakra

(About one inch below the bottom of the sternum in the fleshy area of the upper belly)

This is an active and often volatile energy center. It is the chakra that expresses the ego, or in other words, the identification with oneself, one's individuality. It is a powerful center that extends itself easily out into the world. It likes to express itself through movement, through intelligence and through social connections. If this chakra is dysfunctional or unbalanced, it often leads to ego-centric behavior, anger, rage, frustration, nausea, digestive problems and toxic overload in the liver. In the local area of the solar plexus resides many organs and this chakra helps to regulate these organs, namely the liver, gallbladder, stomach and spleen.

Solar Plexus Chakra Summery

In Balance, Signs & Symptoms	Out of Balance, Emotional Signs & Symptoms	Out of Balance, Physical Signs & Symptoms
self will, ego, understands the self in the larger order of things, trust	self obsessed, self is ruler of the universe, anger, frustration, intolerance, moral superiority	Diabetes, overweight / underweight, no muscle tone, poor digestion, liver disease,

4th Heart Chakra (In the centre of the chest / sternum)

The heart chakra is the chakra of love, compassion and being able to feel and sense the nature of others. When balanced, you feel open to life, open to new people and accepting of the world as it is. With the heart chakra, when functioning well, you tend to feel your way through life rather than overthink it, overplan or try to intellectualize everything. When the heart chakra is out of balance, there is real difficulty in relating to others, in accepting others, feeling forgiveness or compassion. In some cases, there is a real 'hate' that exists, and this is harmful, mostly to the actual person who is doing the 'hating.' If something annoys you or frustrates you, the best thing you can do is open your heart and just let it in – then it won't bother you anymore.

Heart Chakra Summery

In Balance, Signs & Symptoms	Out of Balance, Emotional Signs & Symptoms	Out of Balance, Physical Signs & Symptoms
Unconditional love, acceptance, sees self in all beings, compassionate	Conditional love, fear of rejection, smothering love, always seeking love "out there," hopelessness,	Heart disease, heart palpitations, anxiety, insomnia, asthma, fatigue

5th Throat Chakra (At the base of the neck)

The throat chakra is the center of communication and it has a lot to do with speaking our truth. The throat chakra is almost always deficient or blocked in most people. I think it is largely due to the Western, mainly English style culture of choosing politeness and avoidance of awkward situations rather than speaking up or confronting someone. When this chakra is under stress, the tone of the voice can be weak, excessively loud, wavering or simply harsh to the ear. When this chakra is balanced and working well, the tone of the voice is soothing and comforting and has a healthy and balancing effect on all those who hear it. It is especially important for this area to be balanced if you use your voice for your work life (e.g., teacher, phone consultant, presenter, singer, etc.)

Throat Chakra Summery

In Balance, Signs & Symptoms	Out of Balance, Emotional Signs & Symptoms	Out of Balance, Physical Signs & Symptoms
Communication of truth, assertive, able to express self clearly	Fear of judgment, oppresses feelings and truths, lies often, unclear in speech, doubts self	Asthma, stiff neck and shoulders, sore throats, ongoing coughing, weak voice

6th Third Eye Chakra (Between the eyebrows)

This is the center of the intellect and of intuition. When this chakra is balanced, great ideas, inventions, and intuitions can easily be received. It's like an opening for great insight and inspiration that allows for rapid personal and spiritual evolution. When this area is out of balance, it often leads to regular headaches, foggy head, eye problems, sinus problems and a real lack of intuition and inspiration. It can be put out of balance through excessive thinking, which affects the whole system, or on the other end of the spectrum, under-thinking, which is most commonly due to dulling the mind with intoxicants and sedative drugs. This tends to lead to a real lack of inspiration in the person and often leads to the person feeling increasingly lost and depressed, as their ability to tap into their intuition has been compromised.

Throat Chakra Summery

In Balance, Signs & Symptoms	Out of Balance, Emotional Signs & Symptoms	Out of Balance, Physical Signs & Symptoms
Intuitive, sees through appearances to see the essence, can go beyond mind intellect, open	Critical, judgmental, overplans, worries, worships the rational intellect and mind, strange beliefs	Eye problems, brain fog, headaches, dizziness,

7th Crown Chakra (Top of the head)

This is the Chakra of highest spiritual truth. This center essentially connects us with all that is, with the universe and each other. It provides us also with great insight and intuition. When balanced, it also brings us a heightened state of energy and a feeling of being protected by the universe, and sense of faith becomes increasingly present. When this chakra is blocked or unbalanced, there is an increased feeling of being alone in the world. The mind can easily become dull or overcritical and judgmental of the world because it has come to shut itself off from its higher knowledge.

Crown Chakra Summery

In Balance, Signs & Symptoms	Out of Balance, Emotional Signs & Symptoms	Out of Balance, Physical Signs & Symptoms
Connection to higher consciousness, understands higher purpose, selfless	Lacks direction in life, confusion, depression, feeling lost, self absorbed, selfish	Headaches, brain fog, lethargy, neurosis, dizziness

The Method

The chakra tapping method explained in this book is divided into two main parts. The first part or the "Set Up" is the part you start with, and we want to acknowledge, the present realities, and/or negativities of the situation. The second part is focused on positive reframing, or developing new, more supportive and positive behaviors.

The Set Up – 1ˢᵗ Part Explained
We don't want to pretend or avoid our experience in this moment; we want to first come to accept what is, to experience what is being experienced. Even if it doesn't feel very nice, it's important to be with it so that we can begin to work with it directly. If we avoid it or run away from it, we can't work on it or heal it deeply. It is always better to first acknowledge how you feel, then, once accepted, we can adjust to it and then potentially move into a better space in the next moment.

Positive Reframing – the 2nd part explained
The second part of the method is where we focus on moving into the next moment with I-higher intention - A higher truth of being, if you like. The powerful thing that I have discovered with using any affirmation style framework is to use "being" statements rather than "thinking" statements. I have discovered that it's more powerful to come at it from a place of "being" rather than a place of "thinking." For example, for "being" you could say something like "I am love" and tap that in or hold it in mind for some time. It's a powerful statement, and one that seems to dissolve most of the thoughts in the mind. As an example of thinking statements, you could say, "I choose to be positive and energized." This statement is good, but it doesn't hold as much power as the "being" statement, and you can easily

feel that. You are coming at it from thought rather than coming at it behind thought, from being.

When we come from being, the "right" thoughts and "right" actions automatically come from that space, without much effort at all. When I say "right," I mean more likewise thought and wise effort or appropriate thought and appropriate effort according to the state of being.

So if we work more with simple, powerful statements that focus on "beingness," then these states help to cultivate a space within that allows all thoughts and actions that come from this space to be "right" thoughts and "right" actions.

Therefore, the aim of this EFT chakra method or any self help processes is to be more in "being" and less in "thinking." When in "being," more space arises within the mind and the body, and for some people new to this, it may feel odd or even frightening because of its unfamiliarity. As a result of this, the mind will initially resist this space opening up. Do not be afraid or concerned. That space you are experiencing is progress toward discovering your true, real self. Cultivate that space; cultivate these states of being and all the anxiety, drama and suffering that tend to diffuse in its intensity to reveal the true light within.

How Often to Practice?

Generally, I would recommend that you tap through one chakra each day for 7 days to get the full spectrum of the treatment. Allowing 24 hours in between each chakra gives your body and energy a chance to settle and integrate. It's likely that you will get results of a shift in body and in mind soon after tapping. The chakra that carries the most dysfunction in us will tend to give us the most noticeable shift when tapped through. It is recommended to return and repeat this process two weeks after the original treatment, and the second time around, you could tap through two or three chakras in one day. This would allow you to get through the second course of treatment in two to three days. This just re-affirms the new energetic pattern into your system. If it is a chronic condition, like chronic pain, then tapping through more often, like every day for two weeks or every second day, is more likely to be suitable. Because everyone is different and we carry around various conditions on multiple levels, there is no blanket treatment process that will work for everyone. Use these suggestions as a guide, and if you feel like doing it more, then please go ahead. However, I would suggest doing it no less than one chakra per day and then revisiting the technique two weeks later.

Because energy rises up from the base chakra, is it generally recommended to start your treatment at the base chakra and then move up from there. If, however, you can clearly feel a part of your body that is manifesting as intense sensation and you know what the chakra is in that part of the body, then go straight to that chakra first to clear the discomfort and reduce its intensity. Once that chakra is settled, then it is best go to the base and move up from there, revisiting the original chakra as you go.

The Tapping Points

We work by tapping a number of points on the body with our fingertips of one hand in a gentle yet firm manner, enough so that it stimulates sensation on the point being tapped. We generally just tap one side of the body, but you can also mix it up and tap the other side of the body when doing multiple rounds. Each of these points is a powerful acupuncture point located on the meridian. Many of the points on the head are actually the end point of a meridian.

There are hundreds of videos on YouTube of people exploring the EFT tapping technique, and so I encourage you to check them out as a way to become more familiar with the potential of this modality.

One video on YouTube I would recommend in particular is by "thetappingman." He explains how to tap each of the points, and he also explains the correct sequence of tapping the points. Please put the following address into your internet browser to see the video. www.youtube.com/thetappingman

On the following page is an illustration of all the points used in EFT. We start at the "Karate Chop" on the side of the hand to set up and then we move to the top of the head, moving down one by one to complete one round at the side of the rib cage.

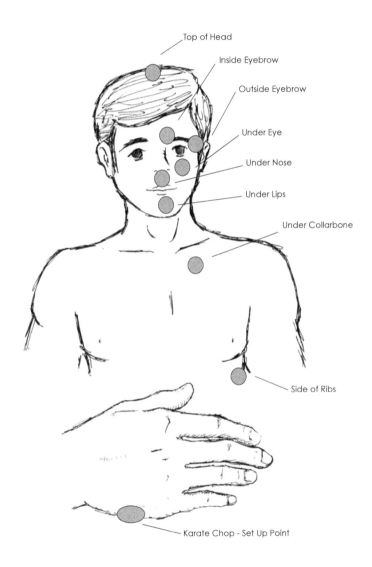

Top of Head

Inside Eyebrow

Outside Eyebrow

Under Eye

Under Nose

Under Lips

Under Collarbone

Side of Ribs

Karate Chop - Set Up Point

The Tapping Points

The Technique Explained

There are two parts to the clearing of each chakra. The first part of the description is information just to help you become more familiar with its function and its multi-level relationships. If one of the emotions, muscles or meridians listed stands out to you in the initial description, then make sure to include those words into your chakra clearing session.

If you have trouble saying the muscle names, then just use the general muscle descriptions, such as hips, legs, etc.

You can mix up the words a little, if you like, to find a way of saying it that feels right for you – just keep working with the keywords listed.

Base Chakra

Governing the Kidney and Bladder Meridians

Emotions: Fear, Anxiety, Insecurity, Doubt, Paranoia, Feeling unsupported

Muscles (general):
Hips
Shoulders
Spine
Calf

Muscles (specific):
Psoas
Illiacus
Upper trapezius
Sacrospinalis
Tibial (anterior and posterior)
Peroneus

Current Truths to Acknowledge and Accept

(Begin the Tapping Here)
Set up - Karate Chop Point:
Even though I may have fear, anxiety, insecurity, doubt or any other emotions stored in my base chakra, I fully and deeply love and accept myself.

Even though I may have pain or tightness in my hips, my shoulders, my spine and my calf muscles, I fully and deeply love and accept myself.

Even though I may have all these emotions, restrictions or blockages in my base chakra, I fully and deeply love and accept myself.

Even though I have all these emotions, restrictions and blockages in my base chakra, I choose to release them from all levels of my being.

(Move the tapping)
Top of the head: Feelings of fear and anxiety
Inside the eyebrow: Insecurity and doubt
Outside of the eyebrow: I love and accept myself anyway.
Under the eye: Any tightness or pain in my hip muscles
Under the nose: My shoulders and spine
Under the lips: I love and accept myself anyway.
Under the collarbone: All these emotions, restrictions and blockages in my base chakra area
Side of the ribs: I now release all of them from all levels of my being.

Repeat and move the tapping x 3

When done…Stop. Drink some water. Take a moment to relax your body and catch your breath. When ready, move on to the second part – Positive Reframe.

Positive Reframe – New Empowering Truths

(Begin the tapping here)
Set up - Karate Chop Point:
Even though I have all those emotions, blockages and pain or tightness in my muscles, I am patient, I am courageous, I am confident.

X2

(Move the tapping)
Top of the head: I am patient
Inside the eyebrow: I am resourceful
Outside the eyebrow: I am able
Under the eye: I am courageous
Under the nose: I am strong
Under the lips: I am confident
Under the collarbone: I am loyal

Side of the ribs: My hip and shoulder muscles are relaxed and free of any pain
Top of the head: My Spine and calf muscles are relaxed and free on any pain
Inside of the eyebrow: All of my calf muscles are relaxed and free of pain
Outside of the eyebrow: I now release any emotional stress from all of these muscles mentioned
Under the eye: My base chakra is balanced and in harmony with all levels of my being
Under the nose: I am aligned with the Highest Good
Under the lips: I am courageous

Repeat and move the tapping x 3

When you have finished your rounds…Relax. Drink some water and take a moment to settle. It is done.

Sacral Chakra

Pericardium Meridian

Emotions: Depression, Worry, Envy, Jealousy, Lust, Hysteria, Inadequacy, Anxiety

Muscles (general):
Buttocks
Hips

Muscles (specific):
Glut max
Glut med
Piriformus
Adductors

Current Truths to Acknowledge and Accept

(Begin the Tapping Here)
Set up - Karate Chop Point:
Even though I may have emotions of jealousy, lust, fear, anxiety or any other emotions stored in my sacral chakra, I fully and deeply love and accept myself.

Even though I may have pain or tightness in my buttocks muscles and my hips, I fully and deeply love and accept myself.

Even though I may have all these emotions, restrictions or blockages in my sacral chakra, I fully and deeply love and accept myself.

Even though I have all these emotions, restrictions and blockages in my sacral chakra, I now choose to release them from all levels of my being.

(Move the tapping)
Top of the head: Feelings of jealousy and fear
Inside the eyebrow: Lust and anxiety
Outside of the eyebrow: I love and accept myself anyway
Under the eye: Any tightness or pain in my buttocks muscles
Under the nose: Any tightness or pain in my hips
Under the lips: I love and accept myself anyway
Under the collarbone: All these emotions, restrictions and blockages in my base chakra area
Side of the ribs: I now release all of them from all levels of my being

Repeat and move the tapping x 3

When done...Stop. Drink some water. Take a moment to relax your body and catch your breath. When ready move on to the second part – Positive Reframe.

Positive Reframe – New Empowering Truths

(Begin the Tapping Here)
Set up - Karate Chop Point:
Even though I have all those emotions, blockages and pain or tightness in my muscles, I am calm, I am relaxed, I am satisfied.

Repeat X2

Move the tapping -
Top of the head: I am calm
Inside the eyebrow: I am tranquil

Outside of the eyebrow: I am complete
Under the eye: I am relaxed
Under the nose: I am satisfied
Under the lips: I am playful
Under the collarbone: I am able
Side of the ribs: All the muscles in my buttocks are relaxed and free of any pain
Top of the head: All the muscles in my hips are relaxed and free of any pain
Side of the eyebrow: I now release any emotions stored from all of these muscles mentioned
Under the eye: My sacral chakra is fully balanced and in harmony with all levels of my being.
Under the nose: I am aligned with the Highest Good
Under the lips: I am satisfied

Repeat and move the tapping x 3

When you have finished your rounds…Relax. Drink some water and take a moment to settle. It is done.

Solar Plexus Chakra

Liver and Stomach Meridians

Emotions: Anger, Rage, Bitterness, Unhappiness, Hostility, Criticism, Disappointment, Nausea, Doubt

Muscles (general):
Chest
Upper back
Neck
Forearms

Muscles (specific):
Pecs
Rhomboids
Levator scapula
Neck flexors and extensors
Brachioradialis

Current Truths to Acknowledge and Accept

(Begin the Tapping Here)
Set up - Karate Chop Point:
Even though I may have emotions of anger, rage, bitterness, unhappiness, discontent, hostility, disappointment, doubt or any other emotions stored in my solar plexus, I fully and deeply love and accept myself.

Even though I may have pain or tightness in my chest muscles, my upper back, my neck muscles and my forearms, I fully and deeply love and accept myself.

Even though I may have all these emotions, restrictions or blockages in my solar plexus, I fully and deeply love and accept myself.

Even though I have all these emotions, restrictions and blockages in my solar plexus, I choose to release them from all levels of my being.

(Move the tapping)
Top of the head: Feelings of anger and rage
Inside the eyebrow: Unhappiness and discontent
Outside of the eyebrow: I love and accept myself anyway
Under the eye: Any tightness or pain in my chest muscles
Under the nose: My upper back and forearms
Under the lips: I love and accept myself anyway
Under the collarbone: All these emotions, restrictions and blockages in my solar plexus area
Side of the ribs: I now release all of them from all levels of my being

Repeat and move the tapping x 3

When done...Stop. Drink some water. Take a moment to relax your body and catch your breath. When ready, move on to the second part – Positive Reframe.

Positive Reframe – New Empowering Truths

(Begin the Tapping Here)
Set up - Karate Chop Point:
Even though I have all those emotions, blockages and pain or tightness in my muscles, I am content, I am fully satisfied, I am in harmony.

X2

(Move the tapping)
Top of the head: I am content
Inside the eyebrow: I am transformational
Outside of the eyebrow: I am open
Under the eye: I am fully satisfied
Under the nose: I am in harmony
Under the lips: I am trusting in the universal way
Under the collarbone: I am accepting
Side of the ribs: My chest muscles are relaxed and free of pain
Top of the head: My upper back muscles are relaxed and free of
any pain
Outside of the eyebrow: The muscles in my neck and forearms
are relaxed and free of any pain
Under the eye: I now release any emotional stress from all of
these muscles mentioned
Under the nose: My solar plexus chakra is fully balanced and in
harmony with all levels of my being.
Under the lips: I am aligned with the Highest Good
Under the collarbone: I am content

Repeat and move the tapping x 3
When you have finished your rounds…Relax. Drink some water
and take a moment to settle. It is done.

Heart Chakra

Heart and Small Intestine Meridians

Emotions: Self doubt, Low self esteem, Low self worth, Insecurity, Anger, Hatefulness, Feeling broken-hearted, Attachment, Shock, Sadness, Nervousness, Ungratefulness

Muscles (general):
Upper back
Belly
Front of legs

Muscles (specific):
Subscapularis
All the abdominals
Quadriceps

Current Truths to Acknowledge and Accept

(Begin the Tapping Here)
Set up - Karate Chop Point:
Even though I may have emotions of hate, self doubt, low self worth, low self esteem, broken-heartedness, attachment, nervousness, sadness or any other emotions stored in my heart chakra, I fully and deeply love and accept myself.

Even though I may have pain or tightness in my upper back muscles, my belly, and my thighs, I fully and deeply love and accept myself.

Even though I may have all these emotions, restrictions or blockages in my heart chakra, I fully and deeply love and accept myself.

Even though I have all these emotions, restrictions and blockages in my heart chakra, I now choose to release them from all levels of my being.

(Move the tapping)
Top of the head: Feelings of hate and self doubt
Inside the eyebrow: Low self esteem and low self worth
Outside of the eyebrow: I love and accept myself anyway
Under the eye: Any tightness or pain in my upper back muscles
Under the nose: My belly and legs
Under the lips: I love and accept myself anyway
Under the collarbone: All these emotions, restrictions and blockages in my heart chakra area
Side of the ribs: I now release all of them from all levels of my being

Repeat and move the tapping x 3

When done…Stop. Drink some water. Take a moment to relax your body and catch your breath. When ready, move on to the second part – Positive Reframe.

Positive Reframe – New Empowering Truths

(Begin the Tapping Here)

Set up - Karate Chop Point:
Even though I have all those emotions, blockages and pain or tightness in my muscles, I am (self) loving, I am grateful, I am joyful.

X2

(Move the tapping)

Top of the head: I am loving
Inside the eyebrow: I am non-attached
Outside the eyebrow: I am complete
Under the eye: I am compassionate
Under the nose: I am worthy
Under the lips: I am secure
Under the collarbone: I am grateful
Side of the ribs: I am confident
Top of the head: I am joyful
Inside the eyebrow: I am passionate
Outside the eyebrow: I am alive
Under the eye: My upper back muscles are relaxed and free of pain
Under the nose: My abdominal muscles are relaxed and free of pain
Under the lips: My thigh muscles are relaxed and free of pain
Under the collarbone: I now release any emotional stress from all of these muscles mentioned.
Top of the head: My heart chakra is fully balanced and in harmony with all levels of my being
Inside of the eye: I am aligned with the Highest Good
Outside of the eye: I am compassionate and loving of others and myself

Repeat and move the tapping x 3

When you have finished your rounds…Relax. Drink some water and take a moment to settle. It is done.

Throat Chakra

Lungs and Large Intestine Meridians

Emotions: Grief, Sadness, Depression, Intolerance, Guilt, Regret, Toxic shame, Inability to let go, Unmerciful

Muscles (general):
Ribs
Shoulders
Lower back
Hips
Hamstrings

Muscles (specific):
Sarratus
Deltoids
Diaphragm
Coracobrachialis
Hamstrings
Fascia latae
Quadratus lumborum

Current Truths to Acknowledge and Accept

(Begin the Tapping Here)
Set up - Karate Chop Point:
Even though I may have emotions of grief, sadness, depression, intolerance, regret, shame, an inability to let go or any other emotions stored in my throat chakra, I fully and deeply love and accept myself.

Even though I may have pain or tightness in my ribs, my shoulders, my lower back, my hips and my hamstrings, I fully and deeply love and accept myself.

Even though I may have all these emotions, restrictions or blockages in my throat chakra, I fully and deeply love and accept myself.

Even though I have all these emotions, restrictions and blockages in my throat chakra, I now choose to release them from all levels of my being.

(Move the tapping)
Top of the head: Feelings of sadness and grief
Inside the eyebrow: Depression and regret
Outside of the eyebrow: I love and accept myself anyway
Under the eye: Any tightness or pain in my ribs, diaphragm and shoulders
Under the nose: My hamstrings, hips and lower back
Under the lips: I love and accept myself anyway
Under the collarbone: All these emotions, restrictions and blockages in my throat chakra area
Side of the ribs: I now release all of them from all levels of my being

Repeat and move the tapping x 3

When done...Stop. Drink some water. Take a moment to relax your body and catch your breath. When ready, move on to the second part – Positive Reframe.

Positive Reframe – New Empowering Truths

(Begin the Tapping Here)

Set up - Karate Chop Point:
Even though I have all those emotions, blockages and pain or tightness in my muscles, I am open, I am able to let go, I am powerful.

X2

(Move the tapping)
Top of the head: I am cheerful
Inside the eyebrow: I am open
Outside the eyebrow: My voice is calm and relaxed
Under the eye: I am merciful
Under the nose: I am compassionate
Under the lips: I am able to let go
Under the collarbone: I am powerful
Side of the ribs: The muscles around my ribs and shoulders are relaxed and free of pain
Top of the head: My hamstring and lower back muscles are relaxed and free of pain
Inside of the eye: My diaphragm is relaxed and pain free
Outside of the eye: I now release any emotions stored in the muscles just mentioned
Under the eye: My throat chakra is fully balanced and in harmony with all levels of my being
Below the nose: I am aligned with the Highest Good
Below the lips: I am able to let go and be free

Repeat and move the tapping x 3
When you have finished your rounds...Relax. Drink some water and take a moment to settle. It is done.

Third Eye

Gall Bladder and Central (Ren) Meridians

Emotions: Feeling overwhelmed, Shy, Shame, Confusion, Disconnected, Anger, Helplessness, Self righteousness, Judgmental, Critical, Bored

Muscles (general):
Front of the shoulder
Back of the shoulder
Behind the knee

Muscles (specific):
Anterior deltoid
Popliteus
Supraspinatus

Current Truths to Acknowledge and Accept

(Begin the Tapping Here)
Set up - Karate Chop Point:
Even though I may have emotions of being overwhelmed, shame, anger, helplessness, feeling judgmental, feeling critical, feeling self-righteous or any other emotions stored in my third eye chakra, I fully and deeply love and accept myself.

Even though I may have pain or tightness in my shoulder muscles around my knee, I fully and deeply love and accept myself.

Even though I may have all these emotions, restrictions or blockages in my third eye chakra, I fully and deeply love and accept myself.

Even though I have all these emotions, restrictions and blockages in my third eye chakra, I now choose to release them from all levels of my being.

(Move the tapping)
Top of the head: Feelings of feeling overwhelmed and helpless
Inside the eyebrow: Anger and feeling judgmental
Outside of the eyebrow: I love and accept myself anyway
Under the eye: Any tightness or pain in my shoulder muscles
Under the nose: The muscles around my knees
Under the lips: I love and accept myself anyway
Under the collarbone: All these emotions, restrictions and blockages in my third eye area
Side of the ribs: I now release all of them from all levels of my being

Repeat and move the tapping x 3

When done…Stop. Drink some water. Take a moment to relax your body and catch your breath. When ready, move on to the second part – Positive Reframe.

Positive Reframe – New Empowering Truths

(Begin the Tapping Here)
Set up - Karate Chop Point:
Even though I have all those emotions, blockages and pain or tightness in my muscles I am clear headed, I am connected, I am humble.

X2

(Move the tapping)
Top of the head: I am connected

Inside the eyebrow: I am clear headed
Outside the eyebrow: I am open
Under the eye: I am loving
Under the nose: I am humble
Under the lips: I am motivated
Under the collarbone: I am assertive
Side of the ribs: I see clearly
Top of the head: My shoulder muscles are relaxed and free of pain
Inside the eyebrow: The muscles around my knees are relaxed and pain free
Outside the eyebrow: I now release any emotions stored in the muscles just mentioned
Under the eye: My third eye chakra is fully balanced and in harmony with all levels of my being
Under the nose: I am aligned with the Highest Good
Under the lips: I am connected to all of life

Repeat and move the tapping x 3

When you have finished your rounds...Relax. Drink some water and take a moment to settle. It is done.

Crown Chakra

San Jiao and Central (Ren) Meridians

Emotions: Despair, Loneliness, Hopelessness, Solitude, Exhaustion, Disconnection

Muscles (general):
Inside of the legs
Calf muscles
Upper back

Muscles (specific):
Gracilis
Sartorius
Teres minor
Soleus
Gastrocnemius
Supraspinatus

Current Truths to Acknowledge and Accept

(Begin the Tapping Here)
Set up - Karate Chop Point:
Even though I may have emotions of despair, loneliness, solitude, exhaustion, disconnection or any other emotions stored in my crown chakra, I fully and deeply love and accept myself.

Even though I may have pain or tightness in my leg muscles and my upper back, I fully and deeply love and accept myself.

Even though I may have all these emotions, restrictions or blockages in my crown chakra, I fully and deeply love and accept myself.

Even though I have all these emotions, restrictions and blockages in my crown chakra, I now choose to release them from all levels of my being.

(Move the tapping)
Top of the head: Feelings of despair and loneliness
Inside the eyebrow: Exhaustion and disconnection
Outside of the eyebrow: I love and accept myself anyway
Under the eye: Any tightness or pain in my leg muscles
Under the nose: Any tightness or pain in my upper back
Under the lips: I love and accept myself anyway
Under the collarbone: All these emotions, restrictions and blockages in my crown chakra area
Side of the ribs: I now release all of them from all levels of my being

Repeat and move the tapping x 3

When done...Stop. Drink some water. Take a moment to relax your body and catch your breath. When ready, move on to the second part – Positive Reframe.

Positive Reframe – New Empowering Truths

(Begin the Tapping Here)
Set up - Karate Chop Point:
Even though I have all those emotions, blockages and pain or tightness in my muscles, I am connected, I am lightness, I am protected.

X2

(Move the tapping)

Top of the head: I am connected
Inside the eyebrow: I am hopeful
Outside the eyebrow: I am open
Under the eye: I am self-realized
Under the nose: I am buoyant
Under the lips: I am lightness
Under the collarbone: I am protected
Side of the ribs: I am united with my Higher Self
Top of the head: All the muscles in my legs are relaxed and free of pain
Inside the eyebrow: My upper back muscles are relaxed and free of pain
Outside the eyebrow: I now release any emotions stored in the muscles just mentioned
Under the eye: My crown chakra is fully balanced and in harmony with all levels of my being
Under the nose: I am aligned with the Highest Good
Under the lips: I am united with all of life

Repeat and move the tapping x 3

When you have finished your rounds…Relax. Drink some water and take a moment to settle. It is done.

Other Methods to Support the Charkas

Yoga Asanas (postures)

Yoga asanas (postures) are powerful practices that work at stimulating, supporting and balancing the energies of the meridians and the Chakras throughout the body and mind. Ont he following pages I have listed a number of yoga asanas that are particularly relevant to the Chakras. You will also find that most postures stimulate and work with at least two chakras at the same time. Results can be enhanced by simply bringing our attention and awareness to the Chakra energy centers while doing yoga postures. Be sure to keep your breath moving when undergoing any asana practice.

If you are new to yoga practices and yoga postures, it is recommended to attend a yoga for beginners course or a number of classes to help you get established in the fundamentals of yoga asana practice.

Base & Sacral Charka

Butterfly – Buddha Konasana
Main benefit – opens the inner legs, opens the back of the body

1. Sitting on the floor or up on some folded blankets, bring the soles of the feet together. Give yourself some space between your groin and your feet.
2. Grabbing hold of the feet, inhale to lengthen the spine, exhale to draw your heart space down towards the feet and floor.
3. Allow yourself to move into this pose slowly. When deep in the pose, focus on relaxing the legs and knees towards the floor. Relax the back and draw the head towards the floor, relaxing the back of the neck and shoulder. Close the eyes and breathe here for a few minutes.
4. When you're ready to come up simply roll up slowly back into sitting with a straight back.

Base Chakra & Sacral Chakra

Horse Stance
Main benefit – Strengthens and grounds the legs into the earth

1. Stand in the center of your mat
2. Bring your legs wide apart (about 1 leg's length apart)
3. Bring your hands into prayer position; relax the shoulders and keep your arms light.
4. Start to gently squat into your legs, keep the knees working back so you're working the hips open.
5. Once you find a spot where you feel "switched on" and activated through the legs, hold it for some time.
6. Connect with your breath. Gently squeeze Mula Bundha (gently squeeze the anus muscle) and hold the posture.
7. Hold for at least 10 long steady breaths before slowly easing up and coming out of it.

8. Be sure to practice this a few times in each session. It's a great practice to do if you feel too "heady."

Solar Plexus & Heart Chakra

Bridge – Setu Bandha Sarvangasana
Main benefit – Strengthens the back muscles and opens the front of the body

1. Lie on your back on the mat, arms down the side of the body, palms down.
2. Bend your knees, place your feet on the mat close to your buttocks, feet hip width apart.
3. As you inhale, flatten your back into the mat and as you exhale, slowly peel the hips off the floor and towards the sky.
4. When you reach the top, suck your belly in, look down the midline of your body with your head still on the floor. Work the arms and hands gently into the floor and gently squeeze the knees towards each other. The knees do not need to touch; the inner thighs just need to be activated.
5. Find your breath and hold for at least three long breaths.

6. When you are ready, inhale to rise a little higher, then, as you exhale, start to slowly peel your spine back onto the mat. Rest.
7. Repeat this action two to three times.

Solar Plexus & Heart Chakra

Standing Back Bend
Main Benefit –back bend to strengthen the back of body and
open the front

1. Place your hands, onto the lower back with fingers pointing
downwards.
2. Draw the elbows towards each other; suck the belly in before
gently drifting the hips forward and leaning back.
3. Feel the heart and throat open. Only hold for a breath and then
come out.

4. Come out by drawing your torso forward and releasing the arms. Feel free to move the hips around in circles to release and then try again.

Solar Plexus & Heart Chakra

Warrior 2 – Virabhadrasana 2
Main benefit – strengthens the legs and opens the arm channels

1. Bring your legs wide apart. Turn your left toes to the front of the mat and your back toes around 45 degrees.
2. Bring your hands onto your hips to start with and sink into your left knee, making sure that the left knee remains either above or just behind the ankle joint.
3. Get solid and into the legs, tuck the belly in slightly.
4. Extend the arms out at shoulder height with the palms downwards. Soften the shoulder and the elbows so that the energy in the arms can move easily.

5. Gaze down the front arm, extending your energy through the eyes.

8. Stay for a few minutes with a steady breath until you can feel the body sensations intensify.

9. To come out, release the arms and straighten out the legs and release.

10. Repeat on the other side.

Heart & Throat Chakra

Cobra Pose – Bhujangasana
Main Benefit - gentle back bend promoting lower back arch

1. Start by lying on your belly on your mat. Feet hip width apart, tops of the feet flat.

2. Arms just underneath the shoulder or just in front of shoulders.

3. Start pushing the hips gently into the floor and raising the chest and head off the floor without any support from the hands.

4. Then start to add the extra support from the hands to help you raise the torso up to where it works for you. It's different for everybody, so listen to your body and don't aim to do the same height as you see in pictures or videos. You don't have to have your arms straight – the back is the most important, so listen to that!

5. Only stay up for a breath and then come back down onto your belly.

6. This pose is good to repeat throughout the class.

7. At the beginning of a class or routine, only come up a little. When the body is warmed up, then you can go up a bit higher.

Third Eye & Crown Chakra

Meditation

There are many different mediation techniques that one can practice. One of the fundamental practices of meditation is "breath awareness." Breath awareness is a simple yet powerful practice because it helps to establish oneself to live in the present moment.

When you start meditation, it is best to sit for at least five minutes at a time. Then, over time, work your way up to around ten minutes at a time.

1. Take up a comfortable cross-legged position with the spine straight. You can sit in a chair if the floor is not suitable for your body.

2. Relax the hands onto your knees or place them one on top of each other in your lap. When you feel comfortable, come to close your eyes.

3. Place the tip of the tongue onto the top of the mouth and only breathe through the nose.

Bring your awareness to the entry point of the nostrils and come to watch your breath as it moves in, and as it moves out.

4. There is no need to change or control the breath. Just let it come in and out easily and effortlessly.

5. The mind will come in and distract us and so when you discover you have been distracted from the task of watching the breath, don't be hard on yourself. Just accept it and come back to the nostrils to watch your breath.

When you feel you have mastered breath awareness, it would be advisable to seek out a meditation group or teacher so that you can delve deeper into the practice of meditation.

Photo credit: longtrekhom

Other Practices to Support the Chakras and the Overall Life Force Energy

1. Breathe Through the Nose

When at rest, place the tip of the tongue on the top of the mouth, just behind the front teeth and breathe steadily through the nose. Do this often, all the time in fact. Reduce and avoid breathing through the mouth, as breathing through the mouth is a sure way to lose a lot of energy and keep the mind dull. When we place the tongue on the top of the mouth, we are connecting the front (Ren) and the back (Du) meridian channels up. The Ren channel runs up the very front of the body and the Du channel runs up the spine on the back of the body, and the two meet in the mouth.

The benefits of this are:
- Stabilizes breath & nervous system = Clear, calm and steady mind
- Promotes a sense of lightness in the body
- Reduces unnecessary speech (wastes energy)
- Head balances better on the neck
- More steady energy (if you feel tired or fatigued, just sit or lie down and practice this for 15 minutes or so)

If we have a blocked nose most of the time, this is a sure sign of too much phlegm and damp in our bodies. It will take time to clear it, start by reducing phlegmy foods like ice-cream, cheese, milk, bananas, and any deep fried oily foods. Walk, walk, walk! This will help move the phlegm so our body can get rid of it. Walk until the nasal passages begin to clear. We can also use nasal flushes that are available at the chemist or drug stores. They work in a similar way as the practice of the 'neti pot,' which is practiced in yoga. The Yogis use neti pots to flush the toxins out and to invigorate the breath and energetic system. If we can't breath through the nose regularly, it makes it very difficult to get the mind and body to a calm yet energetic state.

2. Sitting

We want to promote the healthy flow of energy through the body, so we must learn to sit properly. It's all to do with the orientation of the hips. When we sit, make sure that the knees are slightly lower than the hips. Allow the hips to roll slightly forward, as this will help create a healthy lower back arch and then the head will need to come back to balance on the shoulder. This is a healthy position for the spine.

The worst posture that is most common around the place is that the tailbone is tucked under and the knees are higher than the hips. The spine curls out and is rounded and the head comes forward. This posture totally shuts down the energy flow through the abdominal cavity and the channels on the front of the body.

Poorly designed furniture is one of the main contributors to this phenomenon. Also, the overuse of computers and the use of smart phones and other electronic gadgets contribute greatly to making our posture even worse. Have regular breaks from the computer and minimize your use of smart phones and electronic gadgets. Getting our sitting posture correct and breathing properly is the simplest and probably the most beneficial step we can take. We can practice it anytime, anywhere and it's free. It does take a little time to establish these practices, but once established, it makes a massive difference to your energy levels.

Having a good posture also exudes confidence. Fake confidence comes from the ego and is not sustainable. Real confidence actually comes from a healthy energy field that is flowing within and all around you. This is what people unconsciously pick up on. They feel and sense a healthy energy field, and having a healthy energy field actually influences everyone around you because it uplifts their energy field also. The opposite sex tends to become more attracted to us because of the energy field. You realize after some time that it's not what you do, say or think that matters so much, it's how well your energy field flows around you and how much you remain in touch with this energy field. When we keep our energy field healthy, life just has a way of working out.

To Summarize:

- Adjusting your posture can easily alter your mood and state of mind.
- Breathing through the nose and resting the tip of the tongue on the top of the mouth is one of the simplest and easiest things you can do to uplift your energy field and clear the mind.
- Cleansing the nasal cavities by using methods like the neti pot will assist in easier breathing and uplift your energy.
- Sitting with the knees slightly lower than the hips helps your back to be straighter when sitting.
- Having regular breaks from the computer reduces stagnation.
- Having good posture automatically uplifts your energy field and generates confidence without effort.

Conclusion

The chakras are powerful, energetic portals that govern and influence many levels of our being. By working with these chakras, and the meridian system, we can easily adjust our condition so that we may be more aligned with the universal flow. When we move toward this universal flow - this state of balance - we not only support ourselves, but we naturally support and heal those around us. Anyone that comes into contact with a balanced being is affected when their energy field recognizes the balanced state and naturally begins to resonate with it, whether they are aware of that or not. So therefore, when we make a sincere effort to become a more balanced and harmonious being, we are actually helping all of those around us, also.

Different healing systems and techniques arise at different points in our lives. As for you reading this book, this EFT through the Chakras technique has arisen for you right now and because of this, give it a chance to let it work for you. I'm positive that you will find it to be a powerful technique that will support you on the next level of your healing journey.

Sign up for the author's New Releases
mailing list and get a free book.

Go here to get started:
www.michaelhetherington.com.au/freebook

Other Books By This Author

The Complete Book of Oriental Yoga
A journey into the 5 elements and yoga for the seasons

How to Do Restorative Yoga
Learn the art of a gentle yoga practice for deep relaxation

Chakra Balancing Made Simple and Easy
How to work with the Chakras for enhanced living

Increasing Internal Energy
Building energy from within to enhance daily life and strengthen
our yoga practice

The Yin and Yang Lifestyle Guide
Yin and yang theory applied to modern living

CPSIA information can be obtained
at www.ICGtesting.com
Printed in the USA
FSHW020150191218
54525FS

9 781494 842604